Liquid

FORK IN THE ROAD

—

WRITTEN BY JEFF PRIES

THOMAS NELSON
Since 1798

NASHVILLE   DALLAS   MEXICO CITY   RIO DE JANEIRO   BEIJING

Published in Nashville, Tennessee. Thomas Nelson is a trademark of Thomas Nelson, Inc.

Published in association with the literary agency of Yates & Yates, LLP, Attorneys and Counselors, Orange, California.

Thomas Nelson, Inc. titles may be purchased in bulk for educational, business, fund-raising, or sales promotional use. For information, please e-mail SpecialMarkets@ThomasNelson.com.

Unless noted otherwise, all Scripture quotations are taken from the New Century Version®. Copyright © 2005 by Thomas Nelson, Inc. Used by permission. All rights reserved.

ISBN: 978-1-4185-3352-6

Printed in China.
08 09 10 11 12 SS 9 8 7 6 5 4 3 2 1

■■■ CONTENTS

▄▄▄ INTRODUCTION

LIQUID

Five episodes. One story.

God's Word is as true today as it was when it was written.

But for too long, we have looked at God's Word and wondered how it could possibly impact our lives. It's one thing to simply read the Bible. It's something different altogether to understand it. Far too often we read these stories about people in an ancient land, and we're left feeling flat. "What's this got to do with me?" We know in our hearts that what we're reading is true, right, and good, but we can't see any real way to apply it.

That's where *LIQUID* comes in.

LIQUID presents true-to-life stories of characters with real problems. Because what's the point in putting together a study of God's Word that doesn't deal with any of the issues we actually face? Along with each chapter in this book is a film, filled with characters that live in our world—the real world. Yet their problems and struggles mirror the same struggles found in stories in the Bible.

Jesus is the master storyteller. He helped people understand, made them contemplate, made them consider. He wasn't afraid to cut a story a couple of ways, as if he was saying, "Let me say it another way, a different way, so you can understand." He often gave answers by asking questions in return, so people would investigate, think, learn. It's how he did it, so it's why we do it. We translate ancient stories into the language of today's culture, and we ask relevant questions to help you discover the truth for yourself.

Whether you're with a small group, or simply by yourself, all we ask is that you take a deep breath, pop in the DVD, and then read through these pages and think carefully about the questions and the Scriptures. These are not questions from the SAT—they don't have definitive answers. They are designed for you to reflect upon based on your perspective. Everyone's discoveries will be different. But that's what's great about God's truth—it's one truth, but it's formed differently around each person.

It's simply about taking in, reflecting, and coming up with something useful for your life. Now at last we have an immediate, portable, relevant way to experience God's Word. A revolutionary new way to study the Bible.

LIQUID. God's Word flowing through your life.

▰▰ FORK IN THE ROAD

A fork in the road . . . it always begs the question, Which way are you going to go? And it's at moments like these that decisions are made. Sometimes the decision is well thought-out. Other times we're forced to decide in a split-second what direction to take.

Whatever the choice, the fork always leads us down a road. We have all had fork-in-the-road moments in our lives. As a matter of fact, there are probably quite a few times a day when we stand at a fork and are faced with decisions: Do we say what we're thinking, or not say it? Do we look, or not look? Do we jump into a relationship, or maybe move on? Take the job, or wait for something better?

As we walk through this series, we're going to stand at different forks in the road, seen through the eyes of David, a great man of God. David, a shepherd boy, was destined to become a powerful king. His life was filled with fork-in-the-road moments. Sometimes David chose the road to greatness. Occasionally his choices took him down the road of heartbreak. Yet in spite of all his failures, weaknesses, and sin, God called David a man after his own heart.

Who of us can't relate? Aren't we all, to one degree or another, living lives of victory *and* defeat?

CHAPTER 1: GIANTS

I've never stood up to a wild animal, never looked down the barrel of a gun. Being in a threatening situation to me is having my wife go out to the movies with her friends and leaving me home with the four kids. Screaming, diapers, and dirty dishes—that's as dangerous as it gets for me. And what do I do? I know what I *want* to do . . . run! But I can't, so I dig deep, hold on, and wait by the front door for the lights of my wife's car to pull into the driveway. I know, I'm a little pathetic. I'm sure you are much braver than I am.

Describe a time when you've been in a
threatening situation. What did you do?

Play video episode now.

What makes a ten-year-old boy act like a man? The two bullies must have seemed rather imposing, twice the young boy's size. They took out the mailbox; what would be next? The little boy looked around and decided that he was going to be a man; that he was going to stand up to the giants. He decided that he was going to be clever, use his resources, and not go at it alone. It's what smart people do: look around, see what they have at their disposal, and use it. It's what brave people do: come to the rescue, stare a challenge in the face, and meet it head-on. We can learn a lot from a ten-year-old boy.

What are the things that young David in the film may have been afraid of, and how did he deal with his fear?

How would you have responded if you were in his situation?

²³ While he was talking with them, Goliath, the Philistine champion from Gath, came out. He shouted things against Israel as usual, and David heard him. ²⁴ When the Israelites saw Goliath, they were very much afraid and ran away.

²⁵ They said, "Look at this man! He keeps coming out to challenge Israel. The king will give much money to whoever kills him. He will also let whoever kills him marry his daughter. And his father's family will not have to pay taxes in Israel."

²⁶ David asked the men who stood near him, "What will be done to reward the man who kills this Philistine and takes away the shame from Israel? Who does this uncircumcised Philistine think he is? Does he think he can speak against the armies of the living God?"

²⁷ The Israelites told David what would be done for the man who would kill Goliath.

²⁸ When David's oldest brother Eliab heard David talking with the soldiers, he was angry with David. He asked David, "Why did you come here? Who's taking care of those few sheep of yours in the desert? I know you are proud and wicked at heart. You came down here just to watch the battle."

²⁹ David asked, "Now what have I done wrong? Can't I even talk?" ³⁰ When he turned to other people and asked the same questions, they gave him the same answer as before. ³¹ Yet what David said was told to Saul, and he sent for David.

³² David said to Saul, "Don't let anyone be discouraged. I, your servant, will go and fight this Philistine!"

³³ Saul answered, "You can't go out against this Philistine and fight him. You're only a boy. Goliath has been a warrior since he was a young man."

³⁴ But David said to Saul, "I, your servant, have been keeping my father's sheep. When a lion or bear came and took a sheep from the flock, ³⁵ I would chase it. I would attack it and save the sheep from its mouth. When it attacked me, I caught it by its fur and hit it and killed it. ³⁶ I, your servant, have killed both a lion and a bear! This uncircumcised Philistine will be like them, because he has spoken against the armies of the living God. ³⁷ The Lᴏʀᴅ who saved me from a lion and a bear will save me from this Philistine."

Saul said to David, "Go, and may the Lᴏʀᴅ be with you." ³⁸ Saul put his own clothes on David. He put a bronze helmet on his head and dressed him in armor. ³⁹ David put on Saul's sword and tried to walk around, but he was not used to all the armor Saul had put on him.

He said to Saul, "I can't go in this, because I'm not used to it." Then David took it all off. ⁴⁰ He took his stick in his hand and chose five smooth stones from a stream. He put them in his shepherd's bag and grabbed his sling. Then he went to meet the Philistine.

⁴¹ At the same time, the Philistine was coming closer to David. The man who held his shield walked in front of him. ⁴² When Goliath looked at David and saw that he was only a boy, tanned and handsome, he looked down on David with disgust. ⁴³ He said, "Do you think I am a dog,

that you come at me with a stick?" He used his gods' names to curse David. [44] He said to David, "Come here. I'll feed your body to the birds of the air and the wild animals!"

[45] But David said to him, "You come to me using a sword and two spears. But I come to you in the name of the Lord All-Powerful, the God of the armies of Israel! You have spoken against him. [46] Today the Lord will hand you over to me, and I'll kill you and cut off your head. Today I'll feed the bodies of the Philistine soldiers to the birds of the air and the wild animals. Then all the world will know there is a God in Israel! [47] Everyone gathered here will know the Lord does not need swords or spears to save people. The battle belongs to him, and he will hand you over to us."

[48] As Goliath came near to attack him, David ran quickly to meet him. [49] He took a stone from his bag, put it into his sling, and slung it. The stone hit the Philistine and went deep into his forehead, and Goliath fell facedown on the ground.

[50] So David defeated the Philistine with only a sling and a stone. He hit him and killed him. He did not even have a sword in his hand. [51] Then David ran and stood beside him. He took Goliath's sword out of its holder and killed him by cutting off his head.

When the Philistines saw that their champion was dead, they turned and ran.

What do you learn from this passage about David, Goliath, and the Israelite army? What did each of them bring to the battle?

CULTURAL AND HISTORICAL THOUGHTS:

David, the youngest of Jesse's eight sons, was merely a teenager at the time he faced Goliath. He had already been privately anointed by Samuel as the future king of the Israelites, and had served in Saul's court. David's oldest brothers were engaged in a battle between the Philistines and Israelites, camped across the Valley of Elah. David, tending to his father's flock, made trips to the battlefield, delivering supplies and returning to his father with reports on the condition of his brothers.

A common practice of an army in those days was to pit their strongest warrior against the strongest warrior of the enemy. This was one way of avoiding the high cost of battle in bloodshed, because the winner of the fight was considered the winner of the battle. On this particular trip, David found the Israelite army paralyzed with fear as they faced the taunts of a Philistine warrior, Goliath, who stood over nine feet tall and was undefeated in battle. They had been in a standoff for forty days.

Both sides were waiting for the other to attack first. Up to this point, no one had stepped up to fight Goliath, not even Saul, the most likely opponent since he was the tallest of the Israelites.

Giants are everywhere. Physical, emotional, spiritual . . . they are all obstacles that must be dealt with. Every day starts with the thought, *How am I going to manage through the minefield of the giants in my life?* You can deal with these giants in a lot of ways. You can run from them, saying to yourself, "I know you're there, but if I avoid you, then everything will be OK." You can ignore them, pretending they aren't there: "If I don't acknowledge you as a giant, maybe that doesn't make you as big. If I don't acknowledge you, maybe you'll just go away." Or you can face these giants, tackling them with all your might. It will take energy and courage. It might even get ugly. But at least you will be fighting.

What giants do you see people battling today?

How do you see people responding to these giants?

Life presents us with lots of challenging little things, but what's the *big* thing? What's the one thing in my life that is not just a bump in the road, but a big obstacle? I hesitate to talk about it, because sometimes giants can be personal. What are you saying when you share your giant with others? You are admitting that you're scared, that you're not sure if you can handle it. I have to work up the courage to talk about my giant, but I know that once I admit it, it forces me to really do something about it. My biggest giant is worrying about providing for my family. I worry about giving them the things I want to give them. OK, I said it. Now I need to figure out how I'm going to beat it.

What are the giants in your life? Look at the things that David used to defeat Goliath. What will you use to defeat your giants?

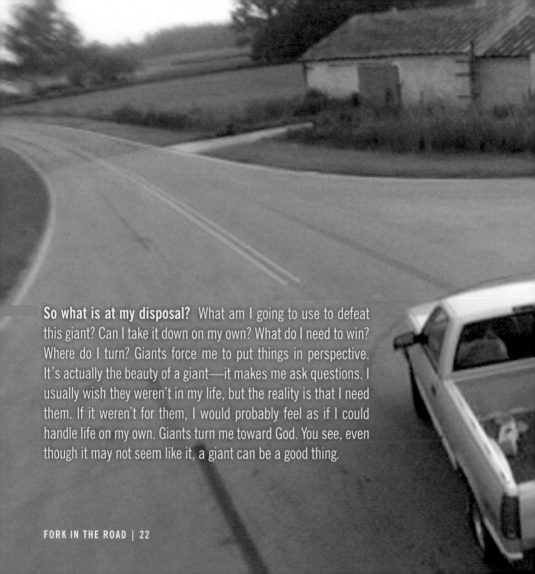

So what is at my disposal? What am I going to use to defeat this giant? Can I take it down on my own? What do I need to win? Where do I turn? Giants force me to put things in perspective. It's actually the beauty of a giant—it makes me ask questions. I usually wish they weren't in my life, but the reality is that I need them. If it weren't for them, I would probably feel as if I could handle life on my own. Giants turn me toward God. You see, even though it may not seem like it, a giant can be a good thing.

What strategies do you need to implement to defeat the Goliaths in your life?

What makes you afraid of the giants in your life?

What can be the danger of not dealing with giants?

Goliath's intimidating stance and attitude beat the Israelite army before the battle even began. How have you seen this happen in the world around you? What are some negative outcomes of giving in to giants?

CHAPTER 2: CONFLICTS

Growing up playing sports, I was always taught to never show emotion. When things are tough, you're never supposed to let the opponent know that you are feeling defeated. Remain expressionless and unfazed. When things are good, keep your excitement under wraps; don't give your opponent anything to feed on. Or better yet, don't get too excited, because after all, this was something you expected to happen. Don't let the highs get too high, and don't let the lows get you down. It's the nature of sports—be emotionless. This "training" has carried over into the rest of my life. If I get emotional, something must be wrong.

What do you do when things get emotional?

Play video episode now.

A classic battle: two men, unable to communicate their way through a disagreement. A peacekeeping woman comes to the rescue. This episode might have really gotten interesting if Abigail had not stepped in. Would it have led to a fistfight? Who would have won? I kind of wish I had gotten to see them fight. I say that now, but that's not really what I would want. I like harmony; I like people being connected. Like Abigail, I am uncomfortable with conflict. What about you?

What is the point of view of each of the characters in the film?

How does each react?

With which character do you most identify?

[10] He answered them, "Who is David? Who is this son of Jesse? Many slaves are running away from their masters today! [11] I have bread and water, and I have meat that I killed for my servants who cut the wool. But I won't give it to men I don't know."

[12] David's men went back and told him all Nabal had said. [13] Then David said to them, "Put on your swords!" So they put on their swords, and David put on his also. About four hundred men went with David, but two hundred men stayed with the supplies.

[14] One of Nabal's servants said to Abigail, Nabal's wife, "David sent messengers from the desert to greet our master, but Nabal insulted them. [15] These men were very good to us. They did not harm us. They stole nothing from us during all the time we were out in the field with them. [16] Night and day they protected us. They were like a wall around us while we were with them caring for the sheep. [17] Now think about it, and decide what you can do. Terrible trouble is coming to our master and all his family. Nabal is such a wicked man that no one can even talk to him."

[18] Abigail hurried. She took two hundred loaves of bread, two leather bags full of wine, five cooked sheep, a bushel of cooked grain, a hundred cakes of raisins, and two hundred cakes of pressed figs and put all these on donkeys. [19] Then she told her servants, "Go on. I'll follow you." But she did not tell her husband.

²⁰ Abigail rode her donkey and came down toward the mountain hideout. There she met David and his men coming down toward her.

²¹ David had just said, "It's been useless! I watched over Nabal's property in the desert. I made sure none of his sheep was missing. I did good to him, but he has paid me back with evil. ²² May God punish my enemies even more. I will not leave one of Nabal's men alive until morning."

²³ When Abigail saw David, she quickly got off her donkey and bowed facedown on the ground before him. ²⁴ She fell at David's feet and said, "My master, let the blame be on me! Please let me talk to you. Listen to what I say. ²⁵ My master, don't pay attention to this worthless man Nabal. He is like his name. His name means 'fool,' and he is truly a fool. But I, your servant, didn't see the men you sent. ²⁶ The Lord has kept you from killing and punishing anyone. As surely as the Lord lives and as surely as you live, may your enemies become like Nabal! ²⁷ I have brought a gift to you for the men who follow you. ²⁸ Please forgive my wrong. The Lord will certainly let your family have many kings, because you fight his battles. As long as you live, may you do nothing bad. ²⁹ Someone might chase you to kill you, but the Lord your God will keep you alive. He will throw away

your enemies' lives as he would throw a stone from a sling. [30] The Lord will keep all his promises of good things for you. He will make you leader over Israel. [31] Then you won't feel guilty or troubled because you killed innocent people and punished them. Please remember me when the Lord brings you success."

[32] David answered Abigail, "Praise the Lord, the God of Israel, who sent you to meet me. [33] May you be blessed for your wisdom. You have kept me from killing or punishing people today. [34] As surely as the Lord, the God of Israel, lives, he has kept me from hurting you. If you hadn't come quickly to meet me, not one of Nabal's men would have lived until morning."

[35] Then David accepted Abigail's gifts. He told her, "Go home in peace. I have heard your words, and I will do what you have asked." [36] When Abigail went back to Nabal, he was in the house, eating like a king. He was very drunk and in a good mood. So she told him nothing until the next morning. [37] In the morning when he was not drunk, his wife told him everything. His heart stopped, and he became like stone. [38] About ten days later the Lord struck Nabal and he died.

What do you learn about David, Nabal, and Abigail from this story?
What principles for conflict management do you see in this scenario?
How might the story have ended if Abigail had not stepped in?

CULTURAL AND HISTORICAL THOUGHTS:

After confronting and settling the long-standing dispute with Saul, who had been hunting him for years, David and his six hundred men returned to their stronghold in the wilderness of Paran. At this time, a wealthy man from Maon named Nabal had three thousand sheep and one thousand goats grazing in that same area. David and his men set about protecting the livestock and their caretakers from the marauding desert dwellers, and, during their watch, not one man or animal was harmed.

David felt that some compensation was due him and his men for their services. He waited until sheep-shearing time, an occasion of great festivities among sheep masters. David sent ten of his young men to Nabal to solicit gifts of food from him and his small band of warriors as payment for their protection. Asking for payment was not out of the ordinary in these times at all, and the culture of the time also demanded that all travelers, no matter the number, should be offered food. Nabal refused and insulted David and his character.

Have you ever met a person and thought, *Wow, we're going to be great friends,* only to find yourself butting heads constantly? You finally come to realize that being around this person is not fun, and not only do you not want him as a friend, but you don't even want him as an acquaintance. That's one thing about friendship—if it doesn't work, you can just slip away. You can't do that with family. If things are tense, you have to make it work. Businesses can be the same way. Sure, you could bolt, but finding a new job isn't always easy. Sometimes you just endure the conflict. Or better yet, learn how to manage it.

In what business, family, and friendship situations do you see people exhibiting conflict management principles like David, Nabal, and/or Abigail?

I'm an Abigail by nature. I hate conflict. I want everyone to get along. Not only do I want people to get along with me, but I want them to get along with each other. Don't get me wrong, I can be a David and go after something that is rightfully mine, and I can do it with real intensity, but I usually don't want that, because it can be a relationship killer. I can also be a Nabal too—an unappreciative idiot, self-centered, with an "it's all about me" attitude. Even though my nature is to keep the peace, I can easily be any of these three characters. You probably can be too.

When have you been like or had to deal with a David, Nabal, or Abigail in your life?

What can you learn from the way Abigail handled the conflict between David and Nabal?

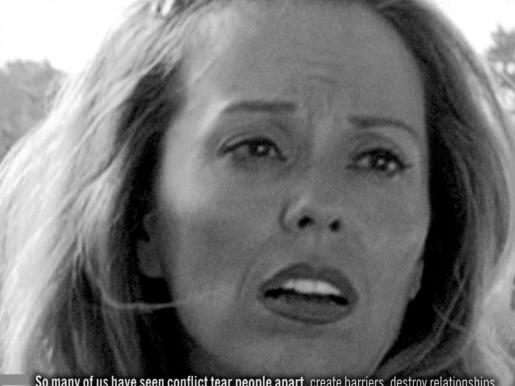

So many of us have seen conflict tear people apart, create barriers, destroy relationships. Maybe we saw it in our parents. We watched them struggle to handle things the right way. We may not have always understood what was going on, but we could sense something was wrong. Our intuition told us that conflict, when handled the wrong way, was something to be avoided. Maybe we saw it in a coach or a teacher or a neighbor. Wherever we saw it, hopefully it was a red flag, a warning, showing us that we didn't want to make the same mistakes.

What conflict are you dealing with in your life right now, and how do you want to respond to it?

When have you seen yourself change when it comes to handling conflict?

What occurrences in your life have shaped the way you deal with conflict?

CHAPTER 3: LURES

Liquid

Buyer's remorse. That little twinge inside that says, *What did I do? Why did I spend that much?* Or the regret you feel when you see something that's just a little better than what you bought. Or the feeling you get when you find out your friend bought the same thing, but for a lot less. Buyer's remorse is inevitable. Soon we're left with a new toy that has lost a little bit of its luster, the bill, and a slight sense of regret.

Describe a time you when bought something you really wanted and then had buyer's remorse.

Play video episode now.

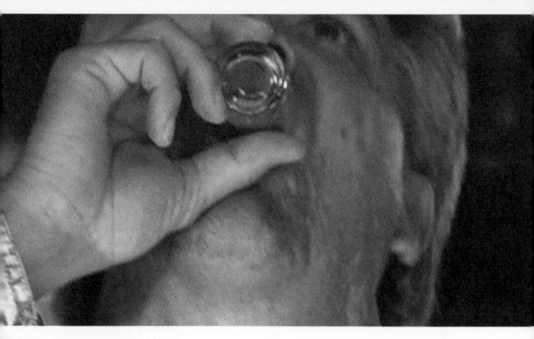

I'm watching this episode, and my mind keeps yelling at David to *stop!* We know he has a drinking problem. We know he shouldn't go to the bar. We know that when the girl gives him that "look," he shouldn't bite. We know he shouldn't take a drink . . . and another . . . and another. We know he should see the signs. We know, we know, we know. It's so easy when we're looking at someone else. Everything is so clear, such a "no-brainer." But telling ourselves to stop, now that's a little more difficult . . .

What "red flags" did David ignore in this episode?

At what points could he still have walked away?

[1] In the spring, when the kings normally went out to war, David sent out Joab, his servants, and all the Israelites. They destroyed the Ammonites and attacked the city of Rabbah. But David stayed in Jerusalem. [2] One evening David got up from his bed and walked around on the roof of his palace. While he was on the roof, he saw a woman bathing. She was very beautiful. [3] So David sent his servants to find out who she was. A servant answered, "That woman is Bathsheba daughter of Eliam. She is the wife of Uriah the Hittite." [4] So David sent messengers to bring Bathsheba to him. When she came to him, he had sexual relations with her. (Now Bathsheba had purified herself from her monthly period.) Then she went back to her house. [5] But Bathsheba became pregnant and sent word to David, saying, "I am pregnant."

[6] So David sent a message to Joab: "Send Uriah the Hittite to me." And Joab sent Uriah to David. [7] When Uriah came to him, David asked him how Joab was, how the soldiers were, and how the war was going. [8] Then David said to Uriah, "Go home and rest."

So Uriah left the palace, and the king sent a gift to him. [9] But Uriah did not go home. Instead, he slept outside the door of the palace as all the king's officers did.

[10] The officers told David, "Uriah did not go home.

Then David said to Uriah, "You came from a long trip. Why didn't you go home?"

[11] Uriah said to him, "The Ark and the soldiers of Israel and Judah are staying in tents. My master Joab and his officers are camping out in the fields. It isn't right for me to go home to eat and drink and have sexual relations with my wife!"

[12] David said to Uriah, "Stay here today. Tomorrow I'll send you back to the battle." So Uriah stayed in Jerusalem that day and the next. [13] Then David called Uriah to come to see him, so Uriah ate and drank with David. David made Uriah drunk, but he still did not go home. That evening Uriah again slept with the king's officers.

[14] The next morning David wrote a letter to Joab and sent it by Uriah. [15] In the letter David wrote, "Put Uriah on the front lines where the fighting is worst and leave him there alone. Let him be killed in battle."

[16] Joab watched the city and saw where its strongest defenders were and put Uriah there. [17] When the men of the city came out to fight against Joab, some of David's men were killed. And Uriah the Hittite was one of them.

¹⁸ Then Joab sent David a complete account of the war. ¹⁹ Joab told the messenger, "Tell King David what happened in the war. ²⁰ After you finish, the king may be angry and ask, 'Why did you go so near the city to fight? Didn't you know they would shoot arrows from the city wall? ²¹ Do you remember who killed Abimelech son of Jerub-Besheth? It was a woman on the city wall. She threw a large stone for grinding grain on Abimelech and killed him there in Thebez. Why did you go so near the wall?' If King David asks that, tell him, 'Your servant Uriah the Hittite also died.'"

²² The messenger left and went to David and told him everything Joab had told him to say. ²³ The messenger told David, "The men of Ammon were winning. They came out and attacked us in the field, but we fought them back to the city gate. ²⁴ The archers on the city wall shot at your servants, and some of your men were killed. Your servant Uriah the Hittite also died."

²⁵ David said to the messenger, "Say this to Joab: 'Don't be upset about this. The sword kills everyone the same. Make a stronger attack against the city and capture it.' Encourage Joab with these words."

²⁶ When Bathsheba heard that her husband was dead, she cried for him. ²⁷ After she finished her time of sadness, David sent servants to bring her to his house. She became David's wife and gave birth to his son, but the Lord did not like what David had done.

What decisions led to David's compromises? What were the consequences? How could he have protected himself?

CULTURAL AND HISTORICAL THOUGHTS:

Winters in Israel were rainy, so spring was the time when men went to war. The roads were dry in spring, making travel easier. Throughout David's life, he was with his men when they went into battle, as it was customary for kings to be with their military during time of war. This time, David stayed behind in his palace and sent his men off to fight the Ammonites.

David's palace was higher than all other residences in the city, which provided a view of all other rooftops and courtyards. One day David saw Bathsheba bathing and he inquired into her identity. At this time David had seven wives and ten concubines, yet he sent for Bathsheba, the wife of one of his soldiers.

Bathsheba was the granddaughter of Ahithophel, one of David's chief counselors, and the daughter of Eliam, one of David's chief soldiers. Eliam apparently had been with David from the time he was in the wilderness before he became king (2 Samuel 23). This suggests that Bathsheba was a lot younger than David and that she spent a lot of time at the palace with her family when she was a small girl.

What things lure us into temptation today? The question should really be, What *doesn't* lure us? After all, everything in life seems designed to entice us. And they will use whatever it takes to succeed, and sometimes it doesn't take much. I know what you are thinking—who is "they"? "They" could be a lot of things. But it's bigger than just saying advertisers, alcohol, or certain people. Learn to recognize what—or should I say who—is behind each temptation, and you will quickly learn to run the other way.

What things lure people today, and how can they protect themselves?

We all have scars from times in our lives when we bit the hook of temptation. It's gotten us all. There are times we fall. There are times when we are torn between the "should I" or "shouldn't I" dilemma that goes back and forth in our brains. That's why we call it "temptation." How have I given in? When have I gotten caught? I could tell you stories of my train wrecks, or I could talk about the subtle ways I've given in to temptation that no one knows about. But these stories aren't original. They are as old as sin itself.

When in your past have you taken the bait? What were the ramifications of going after the lure?

I'm not trying to ignore the idea that lures can be exhilarating. They can be fun, they can be exciting, feel good, or even produce a moment of fulfillment. I admit——sometimes lures give us the excitement in life that we are looking for. Sometimes we're bored; we need a high; we just need something to get us through . . . until the next time. There is no denying that these things can seem inviting. But even though we use these as an escape from reality, reality always comes back to bite us.

What do people gain when they bite on the lures?
What do people lose? Which is greater?

What are the things that entice you today?

What potentially could happen if you were to take the bait?

How can you protect yourself?

CHAPTER 4: AVOIDANCES

Liquid

If you back a cobra against the wall, it will rise up and prepare to attack. Its mechanism for dealing with threatening situations is to go on the offensive. It's saying, "Don't mess with me, or you will get more than you can handle." There is no doubt in my mind that I will not be playing the hero; I'm backing down. No, I'm more than backing down—I'm running far and fast. But have you ever heard of playing possum? Possums just lie there and play dead, letting the world go on without them. Their defense mechanism is to make you feel disinterested and walk away. When things get heated for me, I play the possum. It keeps people from disconnecting, from running. The trouble is, which one is more likely to get stepped on?

If you were to describe yourself as an animal during a disagreement or argument, what animal would you be?

Play video episode now.

Have you ever run away from home? Or even thought about it? It crossed my mind a couple of times growing up, but I never went through with it. I was always stopped by the questions, "Where would I go? And for how long?" After all, I couldn't run forever. I guess I would have to eventually swallow my pride and go back. And what if my folks actually let me go and never tried to track me down? Ouch. What would running away really accomplish? It would just add to the problem. Even as a kid I realized this. I guess that's why I always just stood my ground and tried to work things out.

How do the characters in the film influence one another?

How do you see them avoiding their problems?

[21] When King David heard the news, he was very angry. [22] Absalom did not say a word, good or bad, to Amnon. But he hated Amnon for disgracing his sister Tamar.

[23] Two years later Absalom had some men come to Baal Hazor, near Ephraim, to cut the wool from his sheep. Absalom invited all the king's sons to come also. [24] Absalom went to the king and said, "I have men coming to cut the wool. Please come with your officers and join me."

[25] King David said to Absalom, "No, my son. We won't all go, because it would be too much trouble for you." Although Absalom begged David, he would not go, but he did give his blessing.

[26] Absalom said, "If you don't want to come, then please let my brother Amnon come with us."

King David asked, "Why should he go with you?

[27] Absalom kept begging David until he let Amnon and all the king's sons go with Absalom.

[28] Then Absalom instructed his servants, "Watch Amnon. When he is drunk, I will tell you, 'Kill Amnon.' Right then, kill him! Don't be afraid, because I have commanded you! Be strong and brave!" [29] So Absalom's young men killed Amnon as Absalom commanded, but all of David's other sons got on their mules and escaped.

[30] While the king's sons were on their way, the news came to David, "Absalom has killed all of the king's sons! Not one of them is left alive!" [31] King David tore his clothes and lay on the ground to show his sadness. All his servants standing nearby tore their clothes also.

[32] Jonadab son of Shimeah, David's brother, said to David, "Don't think all the young men, your sons, are killed. No, only Amnon is dead! Absalom has planned this ever since Amnon forced his sister Tamar to have sexual relations with him. [33] My master and king, don't think that all of the king's sons are dead. Only Amnon is dead!"

[34] In the meantime Absalom had run away.

A guard standing on the city wall saw many people coming from the other side of the hill. [35] So Jonadab said to King David, "Look, I was right! The king's sons are coming!"

[36] As soon as Jonadab had said this, the king's sons arrived, crying loudly. David and all his servants began crying also. [37] David cried for his son every day.

But Absalom ran away to Talmai son of Ammihud, the king of Geshur. [38] After Absalom ran away to Geshur, he stayed there for three years. [39] When King David got over Amnon's death, he missed Absalom greatly.

What do you learn about David and his family? What situations did they avoid, and what were the rippling effects of their avoidance?

CULTURAL AND HISTORICAL THOUGHTS:

Two years after his affair with Bathsheba, David's firstborn son, Amnon (by Ahinoam) became completely obsessed with sexual desire for his half-sister, Tamar (her mother was Maacah). Amnon was born and raised during David's rise to fame and power. He was a teenage prince when his father sinned with Bathsheba and would have been witness to the death of David and Bathsheba's baby. He grew up watching his father, listening to his father, and emulating his father.

Since marriage to a sister or half-sister was forbidden (Leviticus 18:11), Amnon resorted to trickery, which resulted in the rape of Tamar to satisfy his all-consuming infatuation. Amnon's lust then turned to hate and he threw Tamar out. Throwing Tamar out made it look as if she had made a shameful proposition and there were no witnesses on her behalf. Amnon's crime also destroyed her chances of marriage— since she was no longer a virgin she could not be given in marriage.

Tamar's full brother, Absalom, was also around when David sinned with Bathsheba, and he was also the recipient of David's lackadaisical approach to discipline and parenting. Absalom became as obsessed with taking revenge for the rape as Amnon was with his infatuation of Tamar. Absalom plotted for two years to kill Amnon and eventually carried out his plan. He then escaped to live with his maternal grandfather, the king of Geshur.

There is a reason that people avoid issues. It's just simpler that way. You don't have to deal with the tension, the drama. When you deal with problems, things just get messy. There are always complications. By avoiding issues, we avoid pain; we sidestep the barbed wire; we step over the potential landmines. Running from situations may not work, but it's cleaner that way . . . isn't it?

When have you seen people avoiding situations they need to deal with—in business situations or in relationships with family and friends?

What were the results?

Some people want to deal with their problems, but they just don't know how. I would say 75 percent of the couples I counsel come to me because of one thing—they can't stand each other! Just kidding . . . kind of. They don't know how to deal with conflict, and because they don't know how to deal with the challenges of relationships, they end up not being able to stand each other. Every time they fail to tackle a tough subject, they make a deposit—a deposit of bitterness and resentment. And those two things just lead to more isolation, more hurt. I don't know who came up with the phrase "Deal with it!" but they were right. It's better that way.

When was a time you avoided dealing with a situation? What happened as the result of not dealing with it?

What situation, if any, are you avoiding dealing with today? What would it look like if you faced it instead?

I never saw many of my family's problems growing up—but not because they weren't there. After all, all families have issues. We just dealt with them by keeping them out of sight, hiding them in a back room, locking them in a closet. I don't know why we didn't openly discuss things. What were we afraid of? But come to think of it, my friends' families kept their problems hidden too. And how do I know they had problems like my family did? Because my friends and I talk openly now—we talk about our families. Even though we kept everything hidden, never to be seen, and even worse, never to be dealt with, things have a way of eventually coming out into the open.

How have the family dynamics you grew up with affected your relationships?
How have they affected your relationship with God?

What are some reasons people "avoid" in their lives?
What does avoiding tend to do to people and relationships?

What are some reasons people are unable to confront difficult issues with others?

CHAPTER 5: COMPASSES

Have you ever been in your car and in such a hurry that the people in front of you couldn't seem to go fast enough? You think, *If I just pull up right behind them, they'll get the hint. That will make them put their foot to the pedal.* After all, what are we supposed to do—just be late? Tailgating is just part of the deal when you're running late. Unless you're the one being tailgated. Then it bugs you to no end. When you're the one in a hurry, tailgating is no problem, right? But when someone comes up behind you in a hurry, that's another story.

While driving, what do you criticize other drivers of doing that you yourself do?

Play video episode now.

Sometimes it doesn't take words. Sometimes it can be as simple as throwing a flask on the ground. Like they say when you make a movie, "Show it, don't tell it." Imagine how the dad must have felt hearing the sound of the flask landing in the dirt. That same canteen that he had held in his hands maybe hundreds of times, something that he had turned mistakenly to for comfort, was now used to confront.

What approach does the daughter in the film use with David?

What makes it effective?

[1] The LORD sent Nathan to David. When he came to David, he said, "There were two men in a city. One was rich, but the other was poor. [2] The rich man had many sheep and cattle. [3] But the poor man had nothing except one little female lamb he had bought. The poor man fed the lamb, and it grew up with him and his children. It shared his food and drank from his cup and slept in his arms. The lamb was like a daughter to him.

[4] "Then a traveler stopped to visit the rich man. The rich man wanted to feed the traveler, but he didn't want to take one of his own sheep or cattle. Instead, he took the lamb from the poor man and cooked it for his visitor."

[5] David became very angry at the rich man. He said to Nathan, "As surely as the LORD lives, the man who did this should die! [6] He must pay for the lamb four times for doing such a thing. He had no mercy!"

[7] Then Nathan said to David, "You are the man! This is what the LORD, the God of Israel, says: 'I appointed you king of Israel and saved you from Saul. [8] I gave you his kingdom and his wives. And I made you king of Israel and Judah. And if that had not been enough, I would have given you even more. [9] So why did you ignore the LORD's command? Why did you do what he says is wrong? You killed Uriah the Hittite with the sword of the Ammonites and took his wife to be your wife! [10] Now there will always be people in your family who will die by a sword, because you did not respect me; you took the wife of Uriah the Hittite for yourself!'

[11] This is what the LORD says: 'I am bringing trouble to you from your own family. While you watch, I will take your wives from you and give them to someone who is very close to you. He will have sexual relations with your wives, and everyone will know it. [12] You had sexual relations with Bathsheba in secret, but I will do this so all the people of Israel can see it.'"

[13] Then David said to Nathan, "I have sinned against the LORD."

Nathan answered, "The LORD has taken away your sin. You will not die.

[14] But what you did caused the LORD's enemies to lose all respect for him. For this reason the son who was born to you will die."

[15] Then Nathan went home. And the LORD caused the son of David and Bathsheba, Uriah's widow, to be very sick. [16] David prayed to God for the baby. David refused to eat or drink. He went into his house and stayed there, lying on the ground all night. [17] The older leaders of David's family came to him and tried to pull him up from the ground, but he refused to get up or to eat food with them.

[18] On the seventh day the baby died. David's servants were afraid to tell him that the baby was dead. They said, "Look, we tried to talk to David while the baby was alive, but he refused to listen to us. If we tell him the baby is dead, he may do something awful."

[19] When David saw his servants whispering, he knew that the baby was dead. So he asked them, "Is the baby dead?"

They answered, "Yes, he is dead."

[20] Then David got up from the floor, washed himself, put lotions on, and changed his clothes. Then he went into the LORD's house to worship. After that, he went home and asked for something to eat. His servants gave him some food, and he ate.

[21] David's servants said to him, "Why are you doing this? When the baby was still alive, you refused to eat and you cried. Now that the baby is dead, you get up and eat food."

[22] David said, "While the baby was still alive, I refused to eat, and I cried. I thought, 'Who knows? Maybe the LORD will feel sorry for me and let the baby live.' [23] But now that the baby is dead, why should I go without food? I can't bring him back to life. Some day I will go to him, but he cannot come back to me."

[24] Then David comforted Bathsheba his wife. He slept with her and had sexual relations with her. She became pregnant again and had another son, whom David named Solomon. The LORD loved Solomon. [25] The LORD sent word through Nathan the prophet to name the baby Jedidiah, because the LORD loved the child.

What do you learn about both David and Nathan?
How did Nathan point David in the right direction? What led to David's restoration?

CULTURAL AND HISTORICAL THOUGHTS:

As a prophet, Nathan was required to confront sin, even the sin of a king. He served as a spokesman for God and a trusted adviser to David. It took great courage to confront David with his sin, because he could have had Nathan killed. It also took skill and tact to speak to David in a way that would make him aware of his wrong actions.

Nathan used a parable to show David his sin and to have David himself pronounce that the consequences of that sin should be death. Nathan tells David of the severe consequences of his sins, all of which come true, including the death of his and Bathsheba's child.

It was during this time that David wrote Psalm 51, as he was racked with guilt for committing his many sins. In Psalm 51, it is evident that David has hope in God's forgiveness. He also wrote Psalm 32 during this time.

In the aftermath of September 11, 2001, there were a lot of TV shows depicting the heroic acts of people. Firefighters, police officers, and average citizens all did the same thing—they stepped into harm's way and rescued those in their most desperate moments. What did they give? A guiding hand, a back to jump on, a flashlight to cut through the dark, dusty air. People who reach out to others in their hardest times, who brave great risk in order to offer guidance to those who need it—these people aren't just helpers; they are heroes.

Where do you see examples of people today helping each other find their way?

Where would I be without my friends? There's a group of guys that I grew up with, played sports with, got into all kinds of trouble with. But one of the biggest things they have done is speak into my life. They have pointed me, redirected me during the tough times. And at the moment, I hated them for it. Who were they to tell me? What do they know? Looking back, though, they were right. Looking back, they helped me. No—more than helped me, they saved me. I am where I am in life largely because of my friends.

Describe a time in your life when someone came alongside you (like Nathan) and helped you change direction.

Who is the Nathan in your life today? Who needs you to be their Nathan?

The "redirect." Hockey has it. It's the subtle pass, when the puck barely touches the stick. TV news has it. It's the turn-of-the-head look reporters give each other, meaning, "I'm sending it back to you." The "redirect." And that's what we're talking about—helping people see things in a different way, having a willingness to convey a different point of view. It can be subtle, which is usually the most effective way of redirecting. But it can also be jarring or abrupt. Whether subtle or direct, the most important thing to remember is that in order to be effective, the confrontation first has to work.

When have you seen people who could have used a Nathan in their lives?

What are some of the reasons it can be hard to listen to people speak into your life? Why do you tend to struggle with listening?

What keeps us from being a Nathan? What blesses us when we are a Nathan to someone?

What is an area in your life where you could use some guidance and direction?

LEADER'S GUIDE

◼ NOTE TO LEADERS

As leaders, we have tried to make this experience as easy for you as possible. Don't try to do too much during your time together as a group—just ask and listen, and direct when necessary.

The questions have a flow, a progression, and are designed to get people talking. If you help the group start talking early on, they will continue to talk. You will notice that the questions start out easy and casual, creating a theme. The theme continues throughout the session, flowing through casual topics, then into world affairs, and then they begin getting personal.

When the questions ask about the Bible, spend time there. Dig in and scour the passage. Keep looking. You and your group will discover that looking into the Bible can be fun and interesting. Maybe you already know that, but there will be people in your group who don't—people who are afraid of their Bibles, or who don't think they can really study them.

Remember, we are seeking life change. This will happen by taking God's Word and applying it to your life, and to the lives of the people you are with. That's the goal for each person in the group. Fight for it.

■■■ TIPS

So, are you a little nervous? Guess what—I get scared too. I always have a little apprehension when it comes to leading a group. It's what keeps me on my toes! Here are some things to keep in mind as you're preparing.

Think about your group. How does this week's topic relate to your group? Is this going to be an easy session? Is this going to be a challenge? The more at ease you are with the topic, the better the experience will be for your group.

Go over the leader's material early, and try to get to know the questions. Sometimes there are multiple questions provided at the end of the chapters. These are extra questions that can be used as supplemental questions at any point throughout the discussion. Look over these extra questions and see if any of them jump out at you. Don't feel that you have to address each question, but they are there if you need them. My worst nightmare is to be leading a group and, with thirty minutes still left on the clock, we run out of questions and there's nothing left to talk about . . . so we sit there and stare at one another in painful silence.

Just remember to keep moving through all the questions. The most important goal of this study is to get personal and see how to apply biblical truths to your own life. When you're talking about how a passage plays out in the world today, a common mistake is to not take it deep enough . . . not to push the envelope and move it from what "they" should do to what "I" should do. As a leader, you will struggle with how much to push, how deep to dig. Sometimes it will be just right; sometimes you will push too hard, or sometimes not hard enough. Though it can be nerve-racking, it's the essence of being a leader.

Here are a few more tips:

- Get them talking, laughing, and having fun.
- Don't squelch emotion. Though it may tend to make you uncomfortable, to the point where you'll want to step in and rescue the moment, remember that leaders shouldn't always interfere.
- Jump in when needed. If the question is tough, make sure to model the answer. Try to be open about your own life. Often, the group will only go as deep as you are willing to go.
- When you look in the Bible for answers, don't quit too soon. Let people really search.
- Don't be afraid of quiet.
- Lead the group—don't dominate it.

These are just a few things to think about before you begin.

▰ CHAPTER 1: GIANTS

Describe a time when you were in a threatening situation. What did you do?

A good way to get everyone involved in this question is for you to answer first. You can approach the question like this: "I know one time I was walking to my car in an airport parking lot, and I thought someone was following me . . . " Remember, what you model to the group is very valuable to the direction you want them to go.

What are the things that young David in the film may have been afraid of, and how did he deal with his fear? How would you have responded if you were in his situation?

For a ten-year-old boy, there is a lot to be afraid of. The sheer size of the guys he is up against is intimidating enough. He may have also been afraid for his family. The film sets up a situation that could go in different directions depending on the decisions/reactions of David. Let your group speculate and play off the emotion of the video.

What do you learn from this passage about David, Goliath, and the Israelite army? What did each of them bring to the battle?

Goliath brought to battle his reputation of being a Philistine champion (v. 23) and of being a warrior since his youth (v. 33); he had his shield bearer in front of him (v. 41); he sneered contempt and shouted at David, trying to intimidate him (v. 43) with his sword, spear, and javelin (v. 45).

Goliath intimidated the Israelites because of his stature and reputation; the Israelite army ran away in fear (v. 24); Saul, the king and leader of the Israelite army, had his own armor (v. 38). David brought with him his faith in a God who would rescue him as he had before (v. 37); he brought the weapons he was used to: his shepherd's staff, his sling, and five smooth stones (v. 40). Most importantly, David said, "Today the Lord will conquer you" (v. 46), and then he used Goliath's own sword to kill him (v. 51). David recognized what no one else did: this wasn't a battle of army versus army; it was a battle of God versus the ungodly—and the outcome was inevitable.

There is a lot there. Make sure you dig deep and cover all of the observations in the text.

What giants do you see people battling today? How do you see people responding to these giants in their lives?

Spend several minutes on this question; it sets the stage for the next question. Allow the group to talk about several situations in which they see others facing challenges. It is in these discussions that group members will see the parallel between what's happening in the world around them and what is happening in their own personal lives. Keep in mind that at this point the group should still be talking in generalizations and not personalizing their answers.

People in the world today are faced with many types of giants. Some giants are intimidating because of their size; others are intimidating because of their reputation. Both can seem overwhelming. Here are some of the giants people face: physical giants, such as illnesses and handicaps; emotional giants, such as loneliness and depression; and behavioral giants, such as addiction or hard-to-break habits. Other giants might involve insecurities, overwhelming financial debt, job loss, or stress, or relationship giants, like separation, divorce, or abuse.

People tend to gravitate toward the negative side of issues first. But you don't want them to stay there. Intentionally transition the conversation to a more positive side—the idea of overcoming our giants. To do that you could ask: "In what situations do you see people overcoming giants in their lives?" Some answers might include: someone who's battling cancer and comes out on the winning side after treatment; marriages that triumph over hardships; someone who prevails over an addiction to drugs or alcohol. Examples like these remind the group that we have a powerful God on our side.

What are the giants in your life? Look at the things David used to defeat Goliath. What will you use to defeat your giants?

This question is designed to help group members look inside and apply the truths they're studying to their life circumstances. Model the answer to this personal question as often as you can and to the degree to which you feel comfortable self-disclosing. Remember, don't expect the group to go deep if you are not willing to be vulnerable.

■■ CHAPTER 2: CONFLICTS

What do you do when things get emotional?

This question will automatically stir up emotional feelings in your group. Don't be afraid of that. Getting in touch with those feelings will help the group transition into the study nicely. However, be aware that because of the nature of the question, you are less likely to get everyone to jump into the discussion right away. To get the discussion started, you may need to bring up situations that demand an emotional response, such as: witnessing a fight, watching a suspenseful movie, or seeing a replay of the 9/11 terrorist attacks.

What is the point of view of each of the characters in the film? How does each react? With which character do you most identify?

The scene your group just watched on the screen is full of emotion. It looks as if a fight might ensue. The woman in the car looks uncomfortable and worried. David seems to be in dire straits, and Nabal appears resolute and angry. Help your group members identify their feelings and which characters they seem to sympathize with after watching the opening scene.

What is the situation, and what do you learn about David, Nabal, and Abigail from this story? What principles for conflict management do you see in this scenario?

The teaching in the film touches on several fork-in-the-road experiences in the passage that you will want your group to focus on: instigating arguments, reacting to disagreements, peacekeeping during disputes. All of these issues will be dealt with in this week's discussion that focuses on managing and resolving conflict.

Nabal instigates the conflict by denying David and his men their due payment; he insulted and sneered at them.

David reacted to the conflict by seeking revenge and sending four hundred men to kill Nabal and all the men of his household.

Abigail responded quickly to defuse the conflict. She went to meet David with a peace offering (food and wine), in humility (bowing before him), and with gratitude for what he had done (protected her household and flocks). She made no excuses for her husband's abhorrent and foolish behavior and reminded David of his own love for the Lord and the fact that vengeance belongs to God alone.

David responded to Abigail's kindness and submissiveness with forgiveness and, in the end, thanked the Lord for keeping him from seeking vengeance.

In what business, family, and friendship situations do you see people exhibiting conflict management principles like David, Nabal, and/or Abigail?

Define once again the roles that Nabal, David, and Abigail played in the conflict found in this week's Bible passage. Nabal caused the conflict by withholding what was rightfully David's. David reacted to the conflict and added to it by seeking revenge. Abigail defused the conflict by being a peacekeeper.

We see and experience conflict in every aspect of life. Take, for instance, the workplace. People are like Nabal when they discriminate with pay, or fail to reward people who work hard by going above and beyond what's expected of them. Then think about families. Often one member of the family is more like Abigail than the others and keeps the peace in family situations where one member is causing pain and another member is overreacting. Or consider a relationship in which someone repeatedly reacts rather than listens when someone is pouring his or her heart out.

Where have you been like or had to deal with a David, Nabal, or Abigail in your life?

This question may cause your group members some discomfort, especially if they see themselves as a Nabal, or even David. Reassure your group by reminding them that everyone is like all three of these characters at one time or another.

Examples:

- One of the moms in your group promises her daughter a new outfit as a reward for cleaning her room, but then backs out of the deal when the deed is done. As a diversion tactic, she reminds the daughter that she was late coming home from a friend's house. (She would be a Nabal in this instance.)
- A man in your group is denied a promotion he feels he deserves, so he quits his job, goes to work for a competitor, and takes a number of clients with him. (Here you have David-like behavior.)
- Two friends are quarreling over something one of them said. You step in and remind them of their personal history. (In this case, you would be an Abigail.)

▰▰ CHAPTER 3: LURES

Describe a time you bought something you really wanted and then had buyer's remorse.

Your group will have fun answering this question. Who among us hasn't bought something only to suffer from buyer's remorse? Although this question might stir up some negative emotion in the end, the struggle of buying something and then regretting it is an experience most people will identify and sympathize with. Make this fun. You'll be getting into a heavy subject, so this is the chance for the group to laugh and lighten up.

What "red flags" did David ignore in this episode? At what points could he still have walked away?

The scene your group just watched reveals David's vulnerability. In the previous session, the group became aware of David's struggle with alcohol. Now, as the bartender pushes a drink at him, enticing him to "take the edge off," David pauses momentarily. Will he give in to ease the pain, or turn away and maintain his dignity? Speculating about how he will respond should prove interesting. Some members may think he's weak and will give in. Others will want to believe that his strength will overcome his weakness. The red flags: going to the bar, being out of control, the alcohol, the bartender, the seduction of the bartender, the first drink.

What decisions led to David's compromises in this Scripture passage? What were the consequences? How could he have protected himself?

Spend several minutes on these questions to give your group time to find all of the temptations and ramifications of David giving in to them. Some of his lures are blatant (adultery), others are more subtle (not being at war with his men). Since it is the more subtle sins we have a tendency to struggle with in our own lives, help the group identify these using a follow-up question, such as: "What are some of the less obvious temptations David faced?"

David faced many decisions, and the consequences of his sin affected many. David was a warrior and should have been on the battlefield with his men. Instead, he stayed at home. He watched a woman bathing, lingering to take a second look because of her beauty. Then his lust turned to adultery as he sent for her, slept with her, and got her pregnant. Instead of facing up to what he'd done, David covered up his sin by trying to get the woman's husband to sleep with her. Her husband, Uriah, being a man of honor, refused and insisted on remaining with the other soldiers. When that didn't work, David involved others in a plot to kill Uriah. End result? Murder. Bathsheba became a widow, returned to David, and became his wife, giving birth to their son.

David had many opportunities to stop the downward spiral. He could have turned and walked away when he first spotted Bathsheba bathing. He could have sent Bathsheba home when she arrived, realizing his mistake. David could have sent for Uriah when he learned Bathsheba was pregnant, confessed his sin, and given Uriah special treatment and compensation. David had no safeguards in place. He had all the resources he needed to protect himself from temptation, but he failed to utilize any of them.

What things lure people today, and how can they protect themselves?

Tip: If you are in a coed group, you can divide into two groups (one for men, the other for women) for these last two questions. To talk about temptation and *not* talk about sexual temptation (at least for the guys), would be missing a major component. You will find that individuals respond more openly when they don't have to talk with the opposite sex present.

Everywhere we look, temptation stares us in the face. Print ads as well as television relentlessly feed our hearts and minds. Advertisers get paid a lot of money to lure us. Bigger and better houses, faster cars, prettier women, glamorous clothes, sweeter foods, sexier waitresses—they're all just a glance away.

When in your past have you bitten the bait? What were the ramifications of going after the lure?

This question is designed to get people to start talking about temptation in a more personal way. Talking about struggles you faced in the past is easier than talking about the present. It lets people see the destruction that has been caused by giving in to temptation. Remember, the goal is to get to present-day life, and then open it up to the future. Don't spend too much time talking about the past if you are going to talk about where people are tempted today.

What do people gain when they bite on the lure? What do people lose? Which is greater?

What are the things that entice you today? What potentially could happen if you were to take the bait? How can you protect yourself?

These are the important questions. They are at the end of the chapter, because these questions are optional. Not all groups are ready to answer these questions. It is a big step to get people to talk about how sin can be exciting for a moment, but then can have terrible consequences. It's also very important to have people talk about the areas in which they are enticed today and how they will deal with it. These are hard questions to answer. So read your group. If you don't think they are ready to talk about their temptations today, have them take their temptations to God in prayer.

CHAPTER 4: AVOIDANCES

If you were to describe yourself as an animal during a disagreement or argument, what animal would you be?

This is an easy question for groups. Watch what happens as people answer—they'll either lean toward being an aggressive animal or a tame one. This type of question can be very self-revealing in a fun way. Don't spend too much time here. There's lots of good discussion ahead.

How do the characters in the film influence one another? How do you see them avoiding their problems?

In this week's film, you'll gain insight into the relationship between David and his daughter, Tamara. Encourage your group to share what they observed as they watched the interaction. What were the family dynamics the group noticed?

Read 2 Samuel 13:21–39. What do you learn about David and his family? What situations did they avoid, and what were the rippling effects of their avoidance?

Spend five to seven minutes on this question. Read the question before reading the Bible passage aloud so the group can watch for each member of the family, the situations they avoided, and their rippling effects. Write down the names of the family members and the attributes and situations that involved them so you can refer back to the list and discuss the situations further. Discuss the parenting dynamics, sibling relationships, and how one situation led to the next because things were never dealt with in David's family.

Tip: The teaching portion of the DVD addresses the rape of Tamar by her brother Amnon. This week's study passage begins right after the rape occurred. Since it is not covered in this passage, recap the teaching portion of the DVD to give background to the study, as it is an important piece of the puzzle when discussing avoidances.

Having been together four weeks now, your group may want to talk about some of the causes for David's actions, or lack of them, with his kids (i.e., his own history of sin, how he treated women, his selfishness, etc.).

David was a loving father, but he failed to discipline his children. His son, Amnon, raped his beautiful daughter, Tamar. He should have punished Amnon for what he did. Instead he got angry, but he did nothing. David's other son, Absalom, plotted and killed his half-brother, Amnon. David grieved and mourned the loss of his son but, again, took no action. Both situations caused David great sorrow. David increased his own sorrow because of his failure to act. And by sending Tamar to Amnon and later Amnon to Absalom, David became an accessory to the crime. After three years of mourning the death of Amnon, David wanted to reconcile with Absalom.

Following Amnon's rape of Tamar, Absalom (Tamar's brother and Amnon's half-brother) hated Amon for what he did. There is no evidence in Scripture that tells us Absalom ever dealt with that hate. In fact, Absalom's bitterness and hatred for his brother grew so much that he plotted for two years to murder him, and he finally killed him at a dinner he himself planned. Absalom fled in fear to his grandfather's house.

The rippling effects of David's inaction left behind a trail of fragmented and broken family relationships.

When have you seen people avoiding situations they need to deal with—in business situations or in relationships with family and friends? What were the results?

Explore situations related to business, family, and friendship. Pay close attention to your group's answers. You may notice as they share insights about the "general" population that they are actually disclosing something about their own relationships. Be sensitive to what you hear, and follow up with anyone on a personal level if you feel his or her disclosure warrants it.

Examples: You see people in business harboring resentment over promotions and apparent inequitable salaries, which leads to tense relationships and a lack of "teamwork." In friendships, jealousy and gossip can lead to fragmented relationships and distrust. There are many issues in marriage: spouses decide to avoid talking about feeling unappreciated or dealing with financial issues. The resentment builds over time until finally, in the heat of an argument, everything boils over.

When was a time you avoided dealing with a situation?
What happened as the result of not dealing with it?

What situation, if any, are you avoiding dealing with today?
What would it look like if you faced it instead?

If you think your group is ready to share at a deeper level, model it by answering these questions yourself first—especially the second question, which asks about tough situations they currently face.

How have the family dynamics you grew up with affected your relationships? How have they affected your relationship with God?

What are some reasons people "avoid" in their lives?
What does avoiding tend to do to people and relationships?

What are some reasons people are able to confront difficult issues with others?

Use these questions when and where you feel it is appropriate.

■ CHAPTER 5: COMPASSES

While driving, what do you criticize other drivers of doing that you yourself do?

This will be fun. How often have you honked or yelled at another driver for doing exactly what you've done? It's easy to spot the "splinter" in someone else's eye, but much more difficult to remove the log from our own. Own up and have fun with this question.

What approach does the daughter in the film use with David? What made it effective?

In this week's video scene, Tamara finds the flask in the glove compartment of her father's truck and assumes (or knows) David has been drinking. It should stir some different kinds of emotion in your group as they consider what she might say to him. After all, she is his daughter. Will she feel powerless? Superior? Run away again and use the flask as her justification for doing it? Her actions will likely determine David's reactions. Will he feel attacked? Guilty? Sad? Like a miserable failure . . . again? Let your group speculate about what could follow the opening scene.

What do you learn about David and Nathan?

How did Nathan point David in the right direction? What led to David's restoration?

There is a lot of information in these twenty-five verses. Try to keep your group focused as much as possible on the role Nathan played in getting David to come clean and to repent of his sin.

David's reaction to Nathan's story is key, as is David's sin and his being confronted by it.

Tip: Point out to your group that in 2 Samuel 7, Nathan visited David with a message from God letting him know that the long-awaited Messiah would come from David's lineage. It is important to remind people that despite his sin, David is still an important player in God's plan.

In the first part of the passage, Nathan comes to David to make him face his sins of adultery and murder. By using a parable of a rich man with flocks of his own, taking a pet lamb from a poor man to use as food for a visitor, Nathan gets David to see the action as a terrible sin. David seethed with anger, and then Nathan unveiled the ugly truth: "*You* are the man!" Nathan tells David of God's absolute sadness and disappointment in David's actions. And he tells David about the consequences that will follow, involving his wife and family.

David admits his guilt and confesses that he has sinned against the Lord. Nathan tells David that although the Lord has taken his sin away, he will not die because of it, but his and Bathsheba's son will die. Just as Nathan predicted, David's infant son became ill and died in spite of David's pleading to God for a change of heart. A repentant David worships the Lord and comforts his wife. God shows his love to David and Bathsheba when he gives them another son, Solomon.

Where do you see examples of people today helping each other find their way?

Help your group think of situations where intimacy and trust helped someone realize when he or she got off track and needed to correct his or her path. Discuss how to be a safe person in that kind of situation and what is required to speak the truth in love.

Describe a time in your life when someone came alongside you (like Nathan) and helped you change direction. Who is the Nathan in your life today? Who needs you to be their Nathan?

Model the first part of this question by telling a personal story about someone who helped you see where you were getting off track. Your story could be as common as spending less and less time with your family, or spending more and more money you didn't have. Or maybe it was the friends you were keeping who were influencing you in a negative way.

Tip: This is a great opportunity to talk about how the small group can be a "Nathan" for your members. If your group is new, you may want to talk about how that is a goal for you as a leader—that you want to make your small group a safe place where people can encourage one another as well as hold each other accountable.

When have you seen people who could have used a Nathan in their lives?

What are some of the reasons it can be hard to listen to people speak into your life? Why do you tend to struggle with listening?

What keeps us from being a Nathan? What blesses us when we are a Nathan to someone?

What is an area in your life where you could use some guidance and direction?

Use these questions where you feel appropriate. Remember, some of these questions are talking in general terms, while others are asking about our own lives. Make sure you don't mix the two. First talk about the world, then yourselves. It's an easier progression.

LIQUID would love to thank:

Chris Marcus, for being a producer, designer, editor, and director of photography on the project. You did it all, and we could not have done it without you.

Mariners Church: To the staff and small group department for all of their help and insight into this entire project. And to the congregation and elder board for their prayers and support.

Kenton Beshore, for the beauty of flow questions.

All of the incredible people in North Carolina, who got this whole thing started.

The cast and crew, for the endless hours of hard work and incredible performances.

Aaron and Mark of Tank Creative, for making us sound good.

Cindy Western, for her help in crafting great questions.

Our incredible editor, Kim Hearon, who, to put it simply, had to deal with us. You made it fun.

All the people at Thomas Nelson, for your hard work and expertise.

And we thank God for having his hand on this project and blessing it.